Rookie
Read-About®
Community

A Day with Firefighters

by Jodie Shepherd

Content Consultant

Chief Vinny Coulehan, Ardsley Fire Department, Ardsley, New York

Reading Consultant

Jeanne Clidas, Ph.D.
Reading Specialist

Children's Press®
An Imprint of Scholastic Inc.
New York Toronto London Auckland Sydney
Mexico City New Delhi Hong Kong
Danbury, Connecticut

Library of Congress Cataloging-in-Publication Data
Shepherd, Jodie.
  A day with firefighters / by Jodie Shepherd.
    p. cm. — (Rookie read-about community)
  Includes index.
  ISBN 978-0-531-28951-8 (lib. bdg.) — ISBN 978-0-531-29251-8 (pbk.)
  1. Fire extinction—Juvenile literature. 2. Fire fighters—Juvenile literature. I. Title.
II. Title: Day with fire fighters.
  TH9148.S53 2013
    628.9'2—dc23   2012013356

Produced by Spooky Cheetah Press

1 2 3 4 5 6 7 8 9 10 R 22 21 20 19 18 17 16 15 14 13

Photographs © 2013: Alamy Images/David R. Frazier Photolibrary, Inc.: 8; Getty
Images/Great Art Productions/Photolibrary: cover; iStockphoto/Mark Coffey:
19; Landov/Juan Carlos Ulate/Reuters: 7; Media Bakery: 4, 31 bottom left (Don
Hammond), 24 (DreamPictures); Richard Hutchings Photography: 27; Shutterstock,
Inc.: 12 (Darin Echelberger), 31 bottom right (Jiri Vaclavek), 3 top (John Kasawa),
31 top left (L Barnwell), 11 (mikeledray), 20 (Ron Frank), 31 top right (Tyler Olson);
Superstock, Inc./Barrett & MacKay/All Canada Photos: 23; Thinkstock: 28
(Comstock), 3 bottom, 15 (Hemera), 16 (Ingram Publishing).

Table of Contents

helmet

air mask

ax

gloves

oxygen tank

boots

4

Meet a Firefighter

Firefighters put out fires.
They save people's lives.
They are very brave.

At the Fire Station

The fire station is a big, busy place.
There is always a lot to do, even
when there are no fires to put out.

The fire trucks must be taken care of so they are ready to go at any moment. The equipment must be checked and ready to go, too.

Firefighters practice drills over and over. They must know what to do when there is a fire.

Here to Help!

A call comes in to the fire station.
A house is on fire!

Firefighters hurry to the fire. The truck's siren warns everyone to get out of the way.

Putting Out
the Fire

Fire and smoke are everywhere.
Are there people inside?
Firefighters rush in.

A long ladder reaches way up to the top floor. Everyone is safe!

19

Firefighters spray water on the fire. The water can be in a tank on the fire truck. Firefighters may also attach a hose to a fire hydrant.

Smoke jumpers are trained to fight wildfires. A smoke jumper might parachute out of a plane to reach the fire.

Stay Safe!

Firefighters are teachers, too.
They teach people how to stay
safe in a fire.

If there is a fire, stay low and get out of the house. Stay out! If your clothing is on fire, stop, drop, and roll. Cover your face with your hands.

stop

drop

roll

27

Listen to firefighters. Firefighters are there to help!

Try It! Read the safety tips on page 26 again. Then try them out! Get low and go. Then stop, drop, and roll!

Be a Community Helper!

- Help prevent fires. Do not play with candles, matches, or fire.

- Make sure there are smoke alarms in your house. A grown-up should change the batteries two times a year.

- Have practice fire drills. Know a safe way to exit every room in the house. Decide on a safe place for the family to meet, away from the house.

Words You Know

boots

firefighter

fire truck

hose

Index

Facts for Now

Visit this Scholastic Web site for more information on firefighters:
www.factsfornow.scholastic.com
Enter the keyword **Firefighters**

About the Author

Jodie Shepherd, who also writes under the name Leslie Kimmelman, is an award-winning author of dozens of books for children, both fiction and nonfiction. She is also a children's book editor.